BREAKING

the

CHAINS

of

CANCER

BREAKING
the
CHAINS
of
CANCER

A PRAYER BOOK FOR THOSE
WHO HAVE LOVED ONES
BATTLING CANCER

STEPHANIE CURRY

Copyright

You may email: prayingtobreakchains@yahoo.com for permissions.
Facebook: facebook.com/BreakingtheChainsofCancer
Twitter: YWHBreaksChains

Cover Design by Scott Curry
ISBN 9781515127925

Printed in the United States of America

DEDICATION

For my identical twin sister
Jacqueline Newsom,
*who fought cancer for a year with such
grace, love, and laughter.
Today she is in the arms of Jesus.
I love you.*

For
Sariah,
*Jackie's daughter.
You are a priceless jewel in the eyes of God.
You have a beautiful spirit and God will enable you to
accomplish great things. Know that you are always
remembered and always loved.*

Also, in loving memory of
Iris Otero
Who prayed vigilantly with me for my sister, although she
herself was fighting an unknown battle with cancer.
Today she is in paradise with Jesus.
Thank you for showing me true power and perseverance
in intercessory prayer.

ॐ

TABLE OF CONTENTS

PREFACE

Breaking the Chains of Cancer: A Prayer Book for those Who Have Loved Ones Battling Cancer arose out of my personal experiences after my identical twin sister was diagnosed with cancer. I searched for a prayer book that addressed the needs of those who have a loved one diagnosed with cancer. Not only are solid Christian prayer books few and far between, cancer prayer books are generally written for survivors. I read some of these prayer books written for survivors, but I found my own spiritual journey was very different from that of my sister. I suspect yours will be too. B*reaking the Chains of Cancer* is for the edification of those who may not have cancer themselves but love someone who does.

In going through this cancer journey with my sister, I thought the only possible and acceptable end result of my prayers was her healing. You might be where I was or you might be further along in your spiritual journey, prepared to accept all outcomes at the hands of God. For my sister, physical healing in this life was not to be. Today she is in paradise with our Savior Jesus.

After her passing, I went through a spiritual valley that was a darker journey than the cancer journey had ever been. While my sister fought, I prayed, hoped and had faith God would heal her. I trusted God completely and knew he would answer our prayers. After my sister passed a new journey began, one that stood in stark contrast to the fight against cancer. This was a journey of doubt and darkness. Yet, God drew me close and opened my eyes more and more as to the nature of his hope and his promises. This enabled me to take true ownership of the things I had said I believed.

Throughout this stretch, I learned sometimes God does not give us the understanding we so desperately seek, but he enlarges and grows our faith to continue to put our trust in him because he does all things well. I learned sometimes we may not get the answers to the questions that seem to amass exponentially each day, but we can find supernatural peace in the assurances of God that it is possible to live each day with renewed joy and peace. Most importantly, God taught me the cancer attacking healthy cells throughout my sister's body was not the only battle taking place. In fact, it was one of many. Not only that, the physical battle wasn't even the *chief* battle!

If you are in the beginning of your cancer journey this may seem doubtful. Yet, as the Word tells us, the chief battle is spiritual. We do not fight against flesh and blood, but against rulers and authorities and spiritual forces of evil. Satan is our enemy. An enemy always seeking to attack the people of God through whatever means necessary.

In my own cancer journey with my family, I could see the enemy was attacking us relentlessly and malevolently. The spiritual battle raged with every doctor visit, chemotherapy treatment, CT scan, and emergency room stay. It stirred with every prayer uttered over my sister and stormed when friends and family sought to encourage her with the Word of God.

The enemy was out to steal: steal our peace, steal our prayer time, steal our joy. He was out to destroy: destroy our trust, destroy our hope, destroy our faith. He wanted to chain confusion, doubt, anger and fear to our hearts and minds.

Since the cancer battle is spiritual, healing could not be the ultimate end goal of all my prayers. (Although, I certainly prayed vigilantly for my sister's healing and hoped for it.) The reason why physical healing cannot be the ultimate end goal is that we stop suffering the consequences and experiencing the victories of physical battles at death. Yet, the consequences and victories of spiritual battles are eternal. Therefore, the risks and rewards of spiritual battles are infinitely greater than that of any physical one.

In light of this, I learned to not just pray for healing, but to pray for God's will to take place in my sister's life; for His peace to be upon her; for her to cast all her worry, anxiety, and fear upon her Heavenly Father; for her to draw nearer to God daily. I prayed her faith and love would grow, and that she would know God more and more. Any victories my sister claimed in her spiritual life would be reaped in eternity and the physical losses would eventually be forgotten, even for those of us who loved her. For we, who love her but especially love and serve Jesus as our Lord and Savior, will one day be reunited with her in heaven and the sorrow of today will be forgotten.

I suspect, if you are reading this book, you have a loved one with cancer and are aware at some level you are involved in a spiritual war. All those who love your loved one are involved. Everyone who is praying for them. No one is excused. None of you can back out and say, "I don't want to be here." You *are* here. You have to stand and fight. That much isn't a choice. The choice comes in how you are going to fight.

Will you fight with the full armor of God? Will you remain alert and sober minded? Will you keep praying, praising, and trusting God? Will you allow God to show himself strong in your lives? Will you carry each other's burdens in peace, faith, and love?

Will you allow God to break the chains of cancer?

Stephanie Curry

❧❧

INTRODUCTION

Breaking the Chains of Cancer: A Prayer Book for those Who Have Loved Ones Battling Cancer is a book specifically written to address spiritual needs of those who have a loved one that is battling cancer.

This book is laid out in a topical fashion. Each chapter begins with prayers. All prayers are based upon God's Word, the Bible.

After the prayers you will find "Verses for Prayer, Meditation, & Encouragement," which contains bible verses that are relevant to the topic in the chapter. This section is intended to provide the Word of God so that you may continue to meditate and pray upon his Word, be encouraged in his will, and stand firm on his promises.

Finally, each chapter concludes with a "Reflections" section where space is provided for you to record your own prayers, impressions, thoughts and emotions.

Most of the prayers are written to include yourself *and* your loved one with cancer (who is designated throughout the book as "[Name]"). Some prayers and chapters focus more heavily on your loved one. For example, the chapter on "Healing" includes prayers for the healing of your loved one. "Young Children of Cancer Fighters" includes prayers for the children of your loved one and their well-being.

The rest of this book is largely devoted to *your* spiritual needs as you fight alongside your loved one. For example the chapters on "Fear" and "Faith" address fears that *you* may be facing and how *your* faith is being tested throughout this battle. Although most of the book focuses on *your* spiritual life, the prayers will indeed make mention of your loved ones, as I know they are never far from your thoughts.

As mentioned in the *Preface*, this book was written with the understanding that you are just as much in the center of a spiritual battle as your loved one and the enemy will certainly be attacking you. The prayers in this book are intended as a guide to assist you in standing on the promises of God. The bible verses are provided because God's Word, is a double-edged sword that you may use against the enemy in battle.

Prayerfully, as you go through this book, may you give all your praise, thanksgiving, worries and fears over to Him. This book is in no way intended to take the place of medical advice, treatments, therapies, or counseling. I believe God can and does use all these things to orchestrate healing in our lives. No matter how God orchestrates healing in your loved ones life, you should always be praying.

As a whole, I hope *Breaking the Chains of Cancer* is a great encouragement to you in your spiritual journey. You can come before the throne of grace with boldness and confidence knowing that God has promised he hears all the prayers of His children, according to his will; no matter how short, no matter how silent, no matter how they are worded, or cried, or shouted or whispered, standing or kneeling, walking, or stumbling, our Father hears the voice of his children.

Even if cancer will be the last physical battle your loved one fights on this earth, they have a great victory in Christ. God has promised them a heavenly citizenship,

2

where you and your loved one will be transformed in glory. God has promised them and all who believe in His Son everlasting life.

I want you to know you are not alone. God has promised you he will never leave you or forsake you. He has promised you and your loved one hope and a future. God has promised you will mount up with wings as eagles. God has promised one day there will not be suffering in your life. He has promised to wipe away all your tears and take away all sickness and death, suffering and pain. With God for you, who can be against you?

I hope *Breaking the Chains of Cancer* reminds you that when God gave his Son to die on the cross for your sins, he gave you everything. God left nothing out. He gave you *everything he has* not just so you will finish the race, but so that you will finish victoriously. When you are feeling completely broken and defeated, as if you can't take another step towards the Father, remember this: you *are getting to the finish line.* God didn't move heaven and earth to give His only Son so that you finish the race hanging on to the last shreds of your faith; as if the God of the Universe wasn't upholding you and strengthening you. You *will* get there in and by the full strength and power of God, singing the praises of God, knowing that he has empowered you with all the power of heaven and earth to defeat the enemy.

With each prayer may you break the chains of cancer the enemy seeks to enslave you and your loved one with. May the faith of all in your cancer journey be increased and may you know God more and more each day, with each failure and with each victory. May you know how deeply God loves you and how he gave everything for you to be victorious in every battle you fight, because the battle belongs to the Lord. You are not alone. May you know he goes before you and behind you and protects you on all sides. May every chain be broken and may you rise victorious.

BREAKING THE CHAINS OF CANCER & WALKING IN FREEDOM

 F ather, [Name] has been diagnosed with cancer and has a long journey ahead. I don't know what [Name] is feeling right now, but I pray for your mercy and grace to pour into his/her life. I pray depression and darkness find no resting place upon [Name]; not in his/her heart or household; not in his/her dreams or waking life. I pray [Name] knows the doctors do not have the final word on the quality of [Name]'s life nor its length. Only you, the Lord God Almighty, who stretched out the heavens with your own hands, and knitted [Name] together in the womb, have the final say in [Name]'s life. Only you have the final say as to what is permitted to afflict him/her and for how long.

Remove any dark veils that have fallen over [Name]'s spiritual vision since his/her diagnosis. Support [Name] now and increase his/her faith so he/she is able to turn to you in every moment on this journey, especially in moments of doubt, confusion, and sadness. I pray that [Name] walks with you in every step of his/her journey and experiences the indescribable liberty that is found in Christ Jesus.

 F ather, do not allow [Name] to ever feel or believe cancer is binding him/her and preventing him/her from becoming exactly who you have called him/her to be. Though [Name]'s life may never be the same from this point on, let his/her heart run free in you and experience the boundless joy of your love, peace, and promises of glory. Surround [Name] with your light and let your presence be heavy upon him/her.

Our experiences now, on this earth, are working for us a great reward in glory. I pray that you will give [Name] a supernaturally vivid vision of you. Increase his/her understanding of you and what his/her suffering is compared to eternity. Let him/her see you at work in his/her life. Show [Name] what it means to be transformed into your image so that every moment of his/her journey he/she is able to hold tight to your promises of glory to glory. Give him/her the ability to look intently into the perfect law, finding freedom in its every verse, on every page, and in every echo of scripture in his/her heart, which is [Name]'s calling as a child of God. You are perfect in all your ways God. You are a good Father. Thank you.

Father, the enemy roams the earth like a roaring lion seeking whom he may devour. Yet, your eyes also go to and fro seeking out the faithful that you may strengthen their faith. Empower [Name] and all those praying for him/her to remain vigilant and constantly on alert. Enable me to take up the mantle of intercessory prayer on behalf of [Name]; that I will not stop pouring my heart out to you on his/her behalf; that when you call me to pray I will be willing to do so no matter the time, day or night.

Give [Name]'s loved ones supernatural grace to pray for one another without ceasing, especially for [Name]. Help us throughout this time to continue to praise and glorify your Name and come to you with our whole selves. Remind us, even in this moment, you are our Father; you are the potter and we are the clay. With every experience, you are shaping us, molding us, and perfecting our faith.

☙❧

VERSES FOR PRAYER, MEDITATION, & ENCOURAGEMENT

So if the Son makes you free, you will be free indeed.
John 8:36

This was in accordance with the eternal purpose which He carried out in Christ Jesus our Lord, in whom we have boldness and confident access through faith in Him.
Ephesians 3:11-12

From my distress I called upon the Lord; The Lord answered me and set me in a large place. The Lord is for me; I will not fear; What can man do to me?
Psalm 118:5-6

[B]ut whenever a person turns to the Lord, the veil is taken away. . . [W]e all, with unveiled face, beholding as in a mirror the glory of the Lord, are being transformed into the same image from glory to glory, just as from the Lord, the Spirit.
2 Corinthians 3: 16, 18

Now the Lord is the Spirit, and where the Spirit of the Lord is, there is liberty.
2 Corinthians 3:17

It was for freedom that Christ set us free; therefore keep standing firm and do not be subject again to a yoke of slavery.
Galatians 5:1

Be of sober spirit, be on the alert. Your adversary, the devil, prowls around like a roaring lion, seeking someone to devour.
1 Peter 5:8

For the eyes of the Lord move to and fro throughout the earth that He may strongly support those whose heart is completely His.
2 Chronicles 16:9

For momentary, light affliction is producing for us an eternal weight of glory far beyond all comparison. . . .
2 Corinthians 4:17

And behold, an angel of the Lord suddenly appeared and a light shone in the cell; and he struck Peter's side and woke him up, saying, "Get up quickly." And his chains fell off his hands.
Acts 12:7

But about midnight Paul and Silas were praying and singing hymns of praise to God, and the prisoners were listening to them; and suddenly there came a great earthquake, so that the foundations of the prison house were shaken; and immediately all the doors were opened and everyone's chains were unfastened.
Acts 16:25-26

Beloved, do not be surprised at the fiery ordeal among you, which comes upon you for your testing, as though some strange thing were happening to you; but to the degree that you share the sufferings of Christ, keep on rejoicing, so that also at the revelation of His glory you may rejoice with exultation.

1 Peter 4:12

∞

REFLECTIONS ON WALKING IN
FREEDOM

_____
_____
_____
_____
_____
_____
_____
_____
_____
_____
_____
_____
_____
_____
_____
_____
_____
_____
_____
_____
_____

∝⅊ℭ

GOD'S WILL

Father, you are just and righteous. Everything you have made is good. Your plan and will is perfect. I confess, I often think that it is not. Especially when my loved one suffers. Sometimes I wonder if you know what you're doing. Yet, can the clay say to the potter, 'Why did you make me this way?' Why did you do this to me?' As *your* beloved jar of clay, I know you have made [Name] and I exactly the way you desire, and permitted things to come into our lives for reasons impossible for us to discern completely. Please forgive me for my irreverence and pride. I know, no matter what, you have promised us hope and a future. You are good. You do all things well. Even if that means allowing cancer into our lives. You make all things beautiful. Though, I do not understand why cancer has come into our lives I pray we entrust ourselves to you completely.

You watch over your people with unmatched tenderness and love. You work everything for good for those who love you and are called according to your purpose. Turn this cancer journey into something beautiful for [Name] and myself. Thank you, Father.

Father, it is your will that I am constantly alert and vigilant in prayer, bringing everything (my thoughts, emotions, requests, praises, thanksgiving, and intercession) to you. Build me up in my spiritual life that I can truly pray without ceasing, rejoice continuously, and not be anxious for anything, but rest in you.

I ask you for wisdom Lord. Godly wisdom that will allow me, [Name], and all of us, to make righteous choices as we face upcoming trials and decisions. Increase my faith so that in my asking you for wisdom I believe you will grant it to me and not doubt. I pray that as I walk this journey with [Name], we walk with you before us and behind us and that we walk in love, kindness, and humility. Your grace is certainly enough for us.

Father, a cancer diagnosis can give the illusion [Name] and his/her family will not be able to accomplish the goals and dreams he/she has for his/her life. Yet, this diagnosis should be a call to action for all of us. A call for us to go and serve your people while we still can, to pray more, praise more, give more, hope more.

Show each of us how we can best fulfill the works you created for us to accomplish. Remind us these works are present in each day no matter our condition. Let us rejoice in what our loved ones accomplish for your kingdom, no matter how small the act. We know every act that builds up your kingdom is invaluable. Therefore, I pray you equip [Name] and me in every good thing to do your will and accomplish works that are pleasing to you.

VERSES FOR PRAYER, MEDITATION, & ENCOURAGEMENT

Now the God of peace, who brought up from the dead the great Shepherd of the sheep through the blood of the eternal covenant, even Jesus our Lord, equip you in every good thing to do His will, working in us that which is pleasing in His sight, through Jesus Christ, to whom be the glory forever and ever. Amen.
Hebrews 13:20-21

Rejoice in the Lord always; again I will say, rejoice! Let your gentle spirit be known to all men. The Lord is near. Be anxious for nothing, but in everything by prayer and supplication with thanksgiving let your requests be made known to God. And the peace of God, which surpasses all comprehension, will guard your hearts and your minds in Christ Jesus.
Philippians 4:4-7

And He [Jesus] was saying to them all, "If anyone wishes to come after Me, he must deny himself, and take up his cross daily and follow Me. For whoever wishes to save his life will lose it, but whoever loses his life for My sake, he is the one who will save it.
Luke 9:23-24

Trust in the Lord with all your heart And do not lean on your own understanding. In all your ways acknowledge Him, And He will make your paths straight. Do not be wise

in your own eyes; Fear the Lord and turn away from evil. It will be healing to your body and refreshment to your bones. Honor the Lord from your wealth And from the first of all your produce;
Proverbs 3:5-9

But if any of you lacks wisdom, let him ask of God, who gives to all generously and without reproach, and it will be given to him. But he must ask in faith without any doubting, for the one who doubts is like the surf of the sea, driven and tossed by the wind.
James 1:5-6

But now, O Lord, You are our Father, We are the clay and You our potter; And all of us are the work of Your hand.
Isaiah 64:8

You turn things around! Shall the potter be considered as equal with the clay, That what is made would say to its maker, "He did not make me"; Or what is formed say to him who formed it, "He has not understanding"?
Isaiah 29:16

On the contrary, who are you, O man, who answers back to God? The thing molded will not say to the molder, "Why did you make me like this," will it? Or does not the potter have a right over the clay, to make from the same lump one vessel for honorable use and another for common use?
Romans 9:20-21

"For I know the plans I have for you," declares the Lord, "plans for welfare and not for calamity to give you a future and a hope. Then you will call upon Me and come

and pray to Me, and I will listen to you. You will seek Me
and find Me when you search for Me with all your heart."
Jeremiah 29:11-13

With all prayer and petition pray at all times in the Spirit,
and with this in view, be on the alert with all
perseverance and petition for all the saints. . . .
Ephesians 6:18

Pray, then, in this way: "Our Father who is in heaven,
Hallowed be Your name. Your kingdom come. Your will be
done, On earth as it is in heaven. Give us this day our daily
bread. And forgive us our debts, as we also have forgiven
our debtors. And do not lead us into temptation, but
deliver us from evil. [For Yours is the kingdom and the
power and the glory forever. Amen."]
Matthew 6:9-13

He has told you, O man, what is good; And what does the
Lord require of you But to do justice, to love kindness,
And to walk humbly with your God?
Micah 6:8

REFLECTIONS ON GOD'S WILL

∽

THANKSGIVING AND PRAISE

Father, let me choose to praise you this day and every day that lies ahead of me in spite of my faults, sins, and doubts; despite this cancer journey and the evil that seems to surround us. You are a God of infinite power. You are a loving God. I praise you because you are good. You are just and kind. You are my provider and healer. You are my banner, going before me in battle and marking me with your Name. I praise you because you are the rock of my salvation.

I praise you because you are a shelter from the storm. I praise you because you count every tear and hear every cry. I praise you because you are a God who cares deeply about your children and you share in our suffering and in our triumphs. I praise you because you are always with me and work all things together for good for those who love you and are called according to your purpose in Christ Jesus.

You are from everlasting to everlasting. You are King of kings and Lord of lords. You are all powerful, all knowing, and ever present. You are the Great I Am. You are Jehovah. There is none like you.

Father, I know this battle against cancer and everything that happens as a result are for the good of [Name], my good, and the good of all those fighting alongside [Name], in order that that your grace will spread and we will praise you more and more. I praise you now because you are

19

sovereign in all circumstances, I praise you that you allowed Christ to endure the worst suffering in order that [Name] and I would have a high priest who is able to sympathize with our pain and our weaknesses. I rejoice that though we may suffer a short time you are perfecting our faith and making it more valuable than gold, resulting in praise, glory, and honor to Jesus.

೫

VERSES FOR PRAYER, MEDITATION, & ENCOURAGEMENT

Rejoice always; pray without ceasing; in everything give thanks; for this is God's will for you in Christ Jesus.
1 Thessalonians 5:16-18

For all things are for your sakes, so that the grace which is spreading to more and more people may cause the giving of thanks to abound to the glory of God.
2 Corinthians 4:15

And in that day you will say, "Give thanks to the Lord, call on His name. Make known His deeds among the peoples; Make them remember that His name is exalted." Praise the Lord in song, for He has done excellent things; Let this be known throughout the earth.
Isaiah 12:4-5

In this you greatly rejoice, even though now for a little while, if necessary, you have been distressed by various trials, so that the proof of your faith, being more precious than gold which is perishable, even though tested by fire, may be found to result in praise and glory and honor at the revelation of Jesus Christ; and though you have not seen Him, you love Him, and though you do not see Him now, but believe in Him, you greatly rejoice with joy inexpressible and full of glory, obtaining as the outcome of your faith the salvation of your souls.
1 Peter 1:6-9

21

Worthy are You, our Lord and our God, to receive glory
and honor and power; for You created all things, and
because of Your will they existed, and were created.
Revelations 4:11

Let us come before His presence with thanksgiving,
Let us shout joyfully to Him with psalms. For the Lord is a
great God And a great King above all gods. . . .
Psalm 95:2-3

"For my thoughts are not your thoughts, Nor are your
ways My ways," declares the Lord. "For as the heavens
are higher than the earth, So are My ways higher than
your ways And my thoughts than your thoughts."
Isaiah 55:8-9

For we do not have a high priest who cannot sympathize
with our weaknesses, but One who has been tempted in
all things as we are, yet without sin. Therefore let us draw
near with confidence to the throne of grace, so that we
may receive mercy and find grace to help in time of need.
Hebrews 4:15-16

০৩৪০

REFLECTIONS ON THANKSGIVING AND PRAISE

_____

_____

_____

_____

_____

_____

_____

_____

_____

_____

_____

_____

_____

_____

_____

_____

_____

_____

_____

_____

_____

_____

☙❧

HEALING

Father, you are my God. I love you. Thank you for this day. Thank you that I can come to you in prayer. I know you love [Name] more than I could ever imagine. You know the plans you have for his/her life. You knew him/her even before he/she was born. His/her whole life was laid before you: past, present and future. You know every smile, every tear, every breath. Before it happened you knew every thought, every prayer, every injury. [Name]'s cancer diagnosis certainly does not come as a surprise to you. I know your perfect will encompasses the path that we are all turning towards.

Father, I ask now for healing in [Name]'s life. I pray you send your Word out over [Name]. You promise us that your Word will not return to you void; that it will accomplish what you send it out to accomplish. I ask you to breathe again upon [Name], for in your breath is life. I pray that every cell in [Name]'s body will line up with your Word and your will. I pray that you will stop the cancer from spreading and that it no longer finds a place in [Name]. Cast the cancer out of [Name] in the matchless and powerful name of Jesus.

I pray that through [Name]'s healing, Jesus will be glorified and [Name] will never stop singing your praises. I give all honor and praise to you Lord, for you are mighty to save, and it is only by your Name we are healed.

Father, thank you for the health you have blessed me with and the health of my family. I know the root of all human suffering, pain, and illness is sin. I also know Jesus is our great physician. He is able to heal every infirmity, from blindness to leprosy to cancer to raising people from the dead. Jesus came to conquer sin and death— which He accomplished when he died on the cross. You sent your Son to show us how desperately we need a savior. Yet, we do not despair because you have given us Jesus.

Open our spiritual eyes so that we may see you working in [Name]'s life and our own lives. Reveal to us whether [Name]'s cancer journey is whether God may be glorified in this fallen world or if it is even rooted in [Name]'s own sin. If it is personal sin, speak to [Name] and soften his/her heart so that he/she may confess his/her sins and be healed.

In this time, I pray [Name] is able to lay every aspect of his/her life before you; every emotion, every thought, and every act. Take all the pieces of his/her life, including those of this cancer journey, fear, pain, and past failures, and use them for your glory. Your ways are higher than ours and you work all things together for good for those who love you and are called according to your purpose. Work good in [Name]'s life now and let his/her healing quickly come. Thank you, Father.

Father, you heal people for many reasons, reasons I can never know or count. In your Word, you healed to show your glory and you healed to bring belief to unbelieving hearts. You healed after a person with an illness or disability displayed great faith in you: healing the man with the withered hand, healing the woman with the issue of blood, healing the lame man, and cleansing the leper.

You also heal because of the faith of someone coming to you on behalf of the person with the illness or disability. You healed the paralytic because of the faith of his friends, a servant because of the faith of his master, a daughter because of the faith of her father.

I have faith in Jesus Christ. I know that your Son conquered all sickness, pain, and death. You wrote a death sentence for Hezekiah, by your own hand; but he prayed and asked for more time, and you answered His prayers. I pray for more time for [Name]; I ask that you bless him/her with many more years. I know one day it will be time for [Name] to leave this earth and join you in paradise, yet I pray that time is not now.

I know every good and perfect gift is from you. I pray for you to bless [Name] with the perfect gift of healing in Jesus' Name, for your glorification.

Father, you are a God of healing. You are the creator of life. In your Word you have given us many examples relating to the healing of the sick. Although you healed many, there were many more you did not heal. In your infinite wisdom you have chosen not to heal people in this life and I honor you, for your ways are not my ways, and your thoughts are higher than mine.

There are times in your Word where you healed only one person though there were many others present, as when Jesus chose only one man to heal at the pool of Bethesda.

You have not always healed people instantaneously and miraculously but have also chosen natural means to heal. Paul suggested wine for ailments, and at one point left his companion Trophemus behind, who was recovering from an illness. We do not know why Paul did not lay hands on Trophemus to heal him (or perhaps he did) yet again, I know your will was working.

Elisha, a righteous man, was not healed in this life and passed away from an illness.

Paul himself prayed for his own healing three times and it was not to be.

There are many other examples in your Word like these. I know for all these things I am to praise you. God, your timing is perfect and your will is right and good. I pray as time passes and [Name]'s healing is delayed, for only reasons you know fully, that our faith becomes even stronger and our trust in you greater.

Jesus said that his people *will* suffer. This is one thing all of humanity shares. Yet, when Jesus's people pass through the fire, they will not be burned. When they pass through the river, they will not be overcome. In this time of suffering, I pray [Name]'s friends and loved ones, who love *you*, will be united in Jesus' Name, knowing we are not alone in the fires or rivers of suffering.

Forgive me for times that I have not trusted you and have doubted because of past disappointments or because a prayer was not answered the way I expected.

Help me to truly know with all my heart and being your grace is sufficient for all of us praying and journeying with [Name]. No matter his/her circumstances, I pray [Name] would know you better and draw near to you. Your strength is made perfect in our weakness.

CₛB Chemo and radiation therapy

Father, [Name] is facing the choice of whether he/she is going to undergo chemotherapy/radiation therapy. This is a very difficult decision for [Name]. I pray [Name] will trust in you and seek your perfect will and not lean on his/her own understanding; in doing so, you have promised to make [Name]'s path straight and his/her judgments just and true.

Give [Name] insight and discernment and bless him/her with clarity of mind and peace of heart. I pray he/she will have the complete support of his/her family. I know this treatment can be extremely difficult on the body and I pray for physical strength for [Name]. Also, bless [Name] with the spiritual and emotional strength to live the life you have called him/her to live. I pray that the name of Jesus is glorified in [Name]'s life.

Father, the doctors of [Name] are saying he/she will have to be treated with chemo/radiation therapy. Give the doctors discernment as to the right treatment combinations, dosage, and length of therapy for [Name]. I pray he/she does not have to undergo therapy any longer than is necessary. Use this therapy to heal [Name] of cancer once and for all. Thank you for giving us medicines and treatments to help [Name]. Bless the doctors to work compassionately and diligently in treating [Name]. Ultimately, you are Jehovah Rapha, the God who heals, and it will be by your hand and your power that [Name] is healed.

ℭ Treatment side effects

Father, give [Name] the stamina to endure his/her upcoming treatments. Have mercy upon [Name]. Protect [Name] from unnecessary pain and the extreme discomforts and side effects of this therapy. Even in [Name's] worst moments, let him/her know he/she is not alone; that you are walking with him/her. Bring relief, comfort, and peace to [Name]. Throughout these treatments, I pray [Name] turns to you again and again. Please enlarge his/her heart to understand more of who you are. Lead him/her and guide him/her in your light and let him/her lean ever more on your promises.

ℭ Ending treatment by choice

Father, [Name] has decided to end his/her therapy treatments. Help me and [Name]'s family members to honor his/her decision even if we don't understand it. Help us to understand [Name] did not come to his/her decision lightly but diligently sought your will. Bless us to love [Name] all the more, especially now when he/she needs us most.

Although, [Name] has made this decision, do not let [Name] descend into despair or regret. Give [Name] renewed comfort, vigor, and courage to finish the race you have set out for him/her. Lead [Name] in your will and guide him/her in your perfect love.

ଔ Ending treatment on doctor orders

Father, the doctors are saying treatment is no longer a viable option for [Name]. [Name]'s cancer is no longer responding to treatment and continues to progress. You, God, apportion to each individual as you will. I know you can heal [Name] and I continue to pray that you do so. Yet, if healing is not to be in life of [Name], I also pray for you to strengthen all of us and prepare our hearts and minds for what may be the end of [Name]'s journey on this earth.

In the book of Isaiah you told Hezekiah to put his house in order because he was going to die. Hezekiah did not die, because he prayed for you to give him more time and you did. We do not know what is to come. I ask you to bless [Name] with good judgment to make all necessary preparations and put his/her house in order. I pray, like Hezekiah, we do not lose hope and continue to seek you for healing and blessings in [Name]'s life and that no matter what, the name of Jesus, above all, will be glorified.

ଔ Ending treatment because of remission

Father, we praise the name of the Lord God Almighty who was, is, and is to come. The doctors have told [Name] that he/she is in remission and there is no sign of cancer! Every good and perfect gift is from you and you make all things beautiful! I praise your Name for healing [Name]. You are the one who has provided wisdom to [Name]'s

31

doctors and given him/her the opportunity to go through treatment.

I pray [Name] uses the time you have blessed him/her with to further your kingdom. I pray [Name]'s testimony will bring glory to your Name and bring more people to know you, Father.

We are all filled with such joy and we rejoice in this victory together! Please do not let us forget these moments. Though we know there might be setbacks in the future or other struggles and battles that come our way, let us remember all the wonderful and glorious things you have done for us that richly display your love.

❧ Delirium and hallucinations

Father, go with [Name] where we cannot go. Be with him/her in the deep places of his/her mind. I ask that hallucinations are kept to a minimum and are benign in nature. I pray that at no point in this journey is [Name] swept too far from reality. Yet, no matter where his/her mind takes him/her, I pray it is always on the wings of your Spirit. Protect [Name]'s mind in its vulnerable times from the enemy's attacks. I ask that there are no long-lasting effects on [Name]'s mental processes from the medications, therapy courses, and radiation treatments.

Walk with [Name] in the streets of his/her perceptions and illusions, bringing light, peace and truth to his/her path.

❦ Loss of appetite

Father, [Name]'s appetite has been waning. When we are weak you are strong. Strengthen [Name] now in his/her weakness. Ensure [Name] has access to nutrient dense foods and beverages. Help him/her to be able to eat those things which are essential to his/her continued survival and fight against cancer. Give wisdom and discernment to [Name] and anyone who prepares his/her food that all meals and beverages are healthful and only aid in [Name]'s health and recovery.

Help me and [Name]'s family to be compassionate with him/her and not force him/her to eat when he/she is simply unable. We cannot understand the struggle happening within [Name]'s body and I pray we are patient and kind-hearted towards [Name], his/her feelings and needs, especially when we are exhausted or lack understanding.

I pray that [Name] is not discouraged as his/her own body continues to change and even become unfamiliar to him/her. Bless [Name] to find peace and comfort in your arms. We know you continue to work inside and outside of [Name]'s body. Satisfy and refresh [Name] and revive his/her soul, in the name of Jesus.

❦ Nausea and vomiting

Father, [Name] is experiencing debilitating nausea and vomiting. Father, please hear [Name]'s groaning and provide him/her with relief. Allow him/her to be able to sleep peacefully and without nausea and vomiting all night.

Minister to his/her heart and increase his/her faith. I pray that you aid the doctors in being able to find the most effective medicines in relieving the worst of [Name]'s symptoms. If there is also an alternative method [Name] is able to use to find relief, I pray too that you lead us in the right direction. I pray the nutrients [Name] is able to keep in his/her body are being used as efficiently as possible. Breathe vigor and nourishment into [Name] in this very hour. Praise the name of the Lord.

☙ Sensitivity to light, sound, touch and smells

Father, [Name] has become painfully sensitive to everything around him/her. I'm sure at this point it seems as if [Name]'s very body is acting against him/her. If you are willing, please remove all cups of suffering, however minor, from [Name]'s life including hypersensitive senses.

Bless all of [Name]'s caregivers and family to be considerate of his/her sensitivities. Provide a way for us to continue to serve [Name] and his/her household without adding to [Name]'s discomforts. Let our work be completed quickly and with kind hearts. Let us lift up prayers to you always on behalf of [Name] for every discomfort he/she suffers, even those that may seem small to us but could make the days seem impossible to get through for [Name]. Thank you Father for seeing [Name] and caring for every single hurt he/she experiences.

☙ Surgery

Father, [Name] has an upcoming surgery. I pray for your grace and peace to be upon [Name] and that he/she will be anxious for nothing. I pray there will no fear in [Name] for you are with him/her.

I pray the doctors performing the surgery are placed by your hand. Give them wisdom and discernment before, during, and after the surgery. I pray all medical staff involved are well-rested and vigilant.

Grant strength to [Name], spiritually and physically, to endure the surgery.

I boldly come before you, your throne of grace, and in the Name and by the power of your Son, ask this surgery to be the means you use to speedily bring forth [Name]'s healing. I pray [Name] finds in you a shelter of protection and provision during his/her recovery. Thank you, Lord.

☙ Insomnia

Father, I ask for you to bring rest and peace to [Name], especially at night when suffering can feel so much worse after a troubling day. Let [Name] know that he/she is not alone in the darkness but your Holy Spirit is standing watch alongside him/her. In this knowledge, let [Name] sleep well.

While [Name] sleeps may his/her body recover, may his/her heart minister to him/her, and may your song be with him/her. Please bring comfort to [Name]'s heart, mind, body, and spirit. I praise you that you are with [Name] every moment. I pray your presence will rest upon

[Name] and that you guard his/her nightly thoughts and emotions with your peace. I pray night becomes a sweet reprieve for him/her, where [Name] can rest in the still, refreshing waters of your Spirit.

C3 Treatment induced infertility

Father, [Name] is going through treatment that can cause infertility. You know [Name]'s heart to have children of his/her own. I pray by the name of Jesus and in your power, [Name] does not become infertile as a result of cancer treatment. I pray that you protect his/her reproductive system from damage and that it remains whole and healthy.

Father, [Name] has become infertile as a result of his/her cancer treatments. I pray [Name] does not feel inadequate as a male/female. I pray [Name] does not allow himself/herself to be defined by what his/her body is able and not able to do. I pray [Name] continues to define himself/herself by who you say he/she is: he/she is fearfully and wonderfully made, an incredible work of art; he/she is created in your very image, he/she is the light of the world and loved by you.

I ask that hope doesn't leave [Name]. The inability to have biological children, when his/her family wants them so much, is incredibly painful. Following a cancer journey, I imagine at times it seems almost too much to bear.

Let [Name] know you hear the cry of his/her heart and banish his/her anguish. I pray [Name] will forever hope for the impossible things that become possible when given from your hands.

Bless [Name]'s family to be compassionate and encouraging and speak words of life over him/her. Give [Name] and his/her family wisdom and discernment about what options remain to him/her to expand his/her family.

Fill [Name] with peace as he/she follows the path you have set before them.

Father, you know how deeply [Name] wants children. Please don't let the enemy steal this dream from their family. I know you have given [Name] the desires of his/her heart for a reason. Make a way for them to have children. Whether you miraculously heal and bless [Name] to be able to conceive, or bring a child into their lives through adoption, foster care or other means. Please prepare the way for them now to have children.

Bless [Name] and his/her family to continue to serve Jesus and His church no matter what path you have in store. Guide the family through their grieving process and let your favor be even more evident in their lives.

VERSES FOR PRAYER, MEDITATION, & ENCOURAGEMENT

But for you who fear My name, the sun of righteousness will rise with healing in its wings. . .
Malachi 4:2

So the crowd marveled as they saw the mute speaking, the crippled restored, and the lame walking, and the blind seeing; and they glorified the God of Israel.
Matthew 15:31

They were utterly astonished, saying, "He has done all things well; He makes even the deaf to hear and the mute to speak."
Mark 7:37

Therefore, confess your sins to one another, and pray for one another so that you may be healed. The effective prayer of a righteous man can accomplish much.
James 5:16

And He has said to me, "My grace is sufficient for you, for power is perfected in weakness." Most gladly, therefore, I will rather boast about my weaknesses, so that the power of Christ may dwell in me.
2 Corinthians 12:9

[A]nd He Himself bore our sins in His body on the cross, so that we might die to sin and live to righteousness; for by His wounds you were healed.
I Peter 2:24

As He passed by, He saw a man blind from birth. And His disciples asked Him, "Rabbi, who sinned, this man or his parents, that he would be born blind?" Jesus answered, "It was neither that this man sinned, nor his parents; but it was so that the works of God might be displayed in him.
John 9:1-3

Then your light will break out like the dawn, And your recovery will speedily spring forth; And your righteousness will go before you; The glory of the Lord will be your rear guard.
Isaiah 58:8

REFLECTIONS ON HEALING

∽✦∽

PATIENCE

Father, I praise your Name for every triumph against cancer [Name] experiences, no matter how small they may seem. Open our eyes to see all victories you win for us, little by little.

In your Word you drove out the Israelites' enemies little by little. Your Word tells us if you had driven them out all at once the Israelites would not have been equipped to be proper stewards of the conquered lands and livestock. They would have lost their inheritance. In order to preserve their inheritance, and especially so that your people would not be overcome, you defeated their enemies little by little. This gave the Israelites time to increase in number to handle the blessings coming their way.

Although they had to wait upon you, they trusted your absolute promise they would be victorious, as long as they continued submitting to your will.

Though it might appear as if things are progressing at an agonizingly slow pace in [Name]'s life and that our victories are minor, I praise your Name, that you have a definitive plan for [Name]'s life where [Name]'s spiritual preservation is your utmost concern. You are driving out [Name]'s enemies, both spiritual and physical, little by little.

Often times, I have thought that the enemy was cancer. Yet, your Word reminds me that the enemy can be many things and cancer is not the worst of them.

For the Israelites, faithlessness was the enemy. You did not warn them against sickness or war, but against allowing their love to grow cold for you. You cautioned them repeatedly to remain faithful, obedient, and remember your awesome deeds on their behalf.

I praise your Name that you are *so good* that you do not just require your children to have faith in you, but you have sent your Holy Spirit to assist *our* spirits to do what our flesh cannot.

Assist [Name] in this very moment. I praise you, Lord, that though he/she may be fighting the greatest struggle of his/her life, you are helping him/her to not only remain faithful and obedient but to remember all the great things you have done for him/her so that his/her faith will not fail him/her at critical times.

With you going before [Name] in battle, he/she does not have to worry about anything else, for you will drive out all his/her enemies before him/her, including cancer.

Father, help me to wait upon you. While I am waiting for you to move powerfully in [Name]'s life, I desire to remain watchful in prayer, vigilant in praise, and attentive to your Word. While I'm waiting, open my eyes to any sin that is in my life, home, or relationships. Anything in my life that is devoted to destruction, help me to root it out, so that you may remain with me in all things. Fill me with your Spirit, and enable me to serve [Name] with patience, humility and the humble love of Christ.

০৪৪৩০

VERSES FOR PRAYER, MEDITATION, & ENCOURAGEMENT

I will not drive them out before you in a single year, that the land may not become desolate and the beasts of the field become too numerous for you. I will drive them out before you little by little, until you become fruitful and take possession of the land.
Exodus 23:29-30

So, as those who have been chosen of God, holy and beloved, put on a heart of compassion, kindness, humility, gentleness and patience; bearing with one another, and forgiving each other, whoever has a complaint against anyone; just as the Lord forgave you, so also should you. Beyond all these things put on love, which is the perfect bond of unity. Let the peace of Christ rule in your hearts, to which indeed you were called in one body; and be thankful.
Colossians 3:12-15

Do nothing from selfishness or empty conceit, but with humility of mind regard one another as more important than yourselves; do not merely look out for your own personal interests, but also for the interests of others. Have this attitude in yourselves which was also in Christ Jesus, who, although He existed in the form of God, did not regard equality with God a thing to be grasped, but emptied Himself, taking the form of a bond-servant, and

being made in the likeness of men.
Philippians 2:3-7

Therefore the sons of Israel cannot stand before their enemies; they turn their backs before their enemies, for they have become accursed. I will not be with you anymore unless you destroy the things under the ban from your midst.
Joshua 7:12

"O my lord, if the Lord is with us, why then has all this happened to us? And where are all His miracles which our fathers told us about, saying 'Did not the Lord bring us up from Egypt?' But now the Lord has abandoned us and given us into the hand of Midian." The Lord looked at him and said, "Go in this your strength and deliver Israel from the hand of Midian. Have I not sent you? . . . Surely I will be with you, and you shall defeat Midian as one man."
Judges 6:13-14, 16

ೞ൭

REFLECTIONS ON PATIENCE

_____

_____

_____

_____

_____

_____

_____

_____

_____

_____

_____

_____

_____

_____

_____

_____

_____

_____

_____

_____

_____

YOUNG CHILDREN OF CANCER FIGHTERS

Father, I lift up my hands to you on behalf of [Name]'s little ones. Give [Name] and [Other Parent/Caregiver] guidance, and good judgment as to how much information regarding [Name]'s cancer, treatments, surgeries etc. that they should share with their children. Provide [Name] with the words and analogies that will bless the children to have the greatest understanding of how life is currently changing for them. Provide [Name] the opportunities to talk openly with his/her children. Bless [Name] with God-like sensitivity in approaching his/her children and meeting their needs. I pray the children also have a safe place to vent their emotions, frustrations, anger, and questions and that all their concerns and fears are addressed clearly.

Inspire [Name]'s family to pray together regularly. Bless his/her children to be reassured and comforted. I ask that your Holy Spirit will permeate all discussions involving [Name]'s children so that they hear only what is true. I pray the truth does not engender fear, or panic in their hearts. Let your Spirit rest upon them and bless them to abide in your perfect love and peace. Enlarge their understanding so that they are able to grasp that you, their Heavenly Father, are watching over their whole family and protecting everyone in your perfect love and grace.

Father, I ask that [Name]'s children in no way blame themselves or think they are at fault for their mother's/father's illness. Enable [Name] and other caregivers to guide the children to cast their cares on you and speak to you whenever they feel anxiety, distress, worry, fear, guilt or hopelessness.

I know this spiritual battle deeply impacts them, even if [Name]'s children do not outwardly show signs of anxiety or seem too young to comprehend what's happening around them. Let your Spirit be the coping mechanism, strength, and security blanket the children need to remain spiritually and emotionally healthy. Open the spiritual eyes and ears of the adults in their lives to help these children walk through this journey in the confidence that you are ever-present so they never have to give up hoping and praying.

Reach the deepest parts of their minds and souls and make all things beautiful for them.

Father, I know you love [Name]'s children even more than [Name] himself/herself. Provide support and loving compassionate caregivers for these children as [Name] is unable to give their full parental attention at this time.

Deliver to [Name] all the things he/she needs at this time to care for his/her children. Awaken your people, the Body of Christ, to stand up and pour into [Name]'s family. Whether [Name] needs babysitting, rides for his/her children, cooked meals, homework help, or someone to just spend a fun day with the children, deliver all these things into [Name]'s life and more. Let [Name]'s children know they are well-loved and well-cared for.

Father, as [Name] and his/her family take this journey together I pray you call [Name]'s children close to yourself and no one hinders them from coming to you. Protect these children from maliciousness, bullying, and the harsh words of others. I pray that your people pray over these children and pour words of life, encouragement, and hope into their lives.

Grow their faith as only you can and let them depend upon you. May they know that you are taking care of them and that you hear every one of their prayers. Drive out all fear, anxiety, and distress in [Name]'s children and keep them in your perfect peace. Let their hearts not be troubled but bless them to abide in you. Protect their hearts, minds and souls from the enemy.

ೲ

VERSES FOR PRAYER, MEDITATION, & ENCOURAGEMENT

For I will pour out water on the thirsty land And streams on the dry ground; I will pour out My Spirit on your offspring And My blessing on your descendants; And they will spring up among the grass Like poplars by streams of water.
Isaiah 44:3-4

Then some children were brought to Him so that He might lay His hands on them and pray; and the disciples rebuked them. But Jesus said, "Let the children alone, and do not hinder them from coming to Me; for the kingdom of heaven belongs to such as these." After laying His hands on them, He departed from there.
Matthew 19:13-15

Death and life are in the power of the tongue,
And those who love it will eat its fruit.
Proverbs 18:21

The Lord is not slow about His promise, as some count slowness, but is patient toward you, not wishing for any to perish but for all to come to repentance.
2 Peter 3:9

But I tell you that every careless word that people speak, they shall give an accounting for it in the day of judgment.

For by your words you will be justified, and by your words you will be condemned.
Matthew 12:36-37

You therefore, beloved, knowing this beforehand, be on your guard so that you are not carried away by the error of unprincipled men and fall from your own steadfastness, but grow in the grace and knowledge of our Lord and Savior Jesus Christ. To Him be the glory, both now and to the day of eternity. Amen.
2 Peter 3:17-18

෴

REFLECTIONS ON YOUNG CHILDREN OF
CANCER FIGHTERS

_____

_____

_____

_____

_____

_____

_____

_____

_____

_____

_____

_____

_____

_____

_____

_____

_____

_____

_____

_____

_____

_____

⚜

FINANCES

Father, [Name] needs help with his/her finances. Open your hands to satisfy his/her financial need. I pray that you supernaturally intervene so his/her hospital bills, treatments, medicines, traveling expenses, and all medical expenses are covered. Provide for all other expenses, past, present and future.

As [Name] waits upon you, I pray he/she will not worry. Help him/her not be fearful or anxious regarding his/her financial situation but that he/she will be kept in your perfect peace. Increase [Name]'s faith. Grow his/her confidence in Jesus. Let [Name] praise you in the midst of all these struggles and in every step of the path you have marked for him/her.

For we know you clothe the grass of the field and provide for the sparrows, how much more will you provide for your child, [Name]— the one for whom your thoughts outweigh the number of grains of sand on the earth.

I pray that [Name] will seek you first and your righteousness even in the midst of this tempest. In doing so, I know you will provide for all of [Name]'s needs.

❧ No medical insurance

Father, [Name] does not have medical insurance/ his/her medical insurance is very limited. I pray that this will not be an obstacle to [Name] receiving the best of care including compassionate and excellent doctors and nurses.

I pray that you provide financially for all the needs of [Name] through the Body of Christ and family and friends that are capable of giving. Your Word exhorts us to provide for our family members and to care for our relatives and meet their needs as we are able. If we have the ability to give and do not give, we are considered worse than even those that do not believe. Not giving to your people in need, when we are able, is a great offense to your Spirit. I pray that [Name]'s church family, relatives, friends, and even those that do not know [Name] may be moved to give to help cover [Name]'s medical expenses.

I pray that those who give will give joyfully and with gladness out of the abundance you have blessed them with and in so doing they are blessed even more. Give back to those who bless [Name] even more than they had before, Father.

For those who give *sacrificially*, bless all of *their* needs to be provided so no one is lacking. Bless their children and homes, Father. Thank you for the Body of Christ. There is nothing like her in all the earth. I praise your Name for all those who have sowed into [Name]'s life. You are worthy to be praised.

❧ Difficulties obtaining coverage

Father, [Name]'s insurance company does not want to cover certain treatments or expenses and [Name] has been battling to have his/her expenses covered. Father, I pray that you will intervene in this fight so [Name] may focus on their health and family. I pray, in the name of Jesus, that the insurance company will cover *all* expenses related to

[Name]'s diagnosis, treatments, preventative care, and therapies. I pray that [Name] does not accumulate any medical debt, Father. Supply all of [Name]'s needs according to your riches in glory in Christ Jesus.

❧ Financial strain on the family

Father, in your Word you promise to provide all of our needs according to your riches in glory in Christ Jesus. I am told not to worry about what I will eat or what I will drink or what I will wear. You already know all of my needs and those of [Name] and [Name]'s family. It is for me to eagerly seek first your kingdom and your righteousness and you will bless me with all the things I need.

Help me each day to seek you first. Remind me to do so Lord in times where I allow financial anxiety to take the forefront of my thoughts. I need help leaning on you. By worrying I cannot add not even an hour to my life. So, I cast all my cares upon you because you care for me. Bless me to be a good steward of what you have entrusted to my family and to guard our finances diligently and with great attentiveness.

❧ Prayer for needs generally

Father, I know the riches of our Savior are unparalleled and endless because they come from you. I pray that you meet all the needs of [Name]: financially, spiritually, emotionally, and physically. I pray that the Body of Christ and [Name]'s friends and family will gather around him/her like they never have before.

Open the ears of your people so that they may hear the needs of [Name] even without him/her saying a word. Open the eyes of your people so that they may see the needs of [Name], especially the needs that are not obvious or are unknown.

You call us out to carry each other's burdens in order that we may fulfill the law of Christ. I pray that your people will be moved to carry the burdens of [Name] by praying, providing, listening, and caring for him/her in the love of Christ.

If your people have the supply and [Name] has the need, I pray it will be given to him/her without delay. Whether those in the Body can help with medical bills, childcare, meals, cleaning [Name]'s home, rides, intercessory prayer, and every other need, I pray that your Spirit will hover over all who are able. Move their hearts with compassion and let them allow you to use their hands and feet to bless [Name].

I pray that [Name] will have more than enough to supply his/her needs and the needs of his/her family in this time. Thank you Father.

∞

VERSES FOR MEDITATION, PRAYER, AND ENCOURAGEMENT

And my God will supply all your needs according to His riches in glory in Christ Jesus
Philippians 4:19

Better is the little of the righteous Than the abundance of many wicked.
Psalm 37:16

Owe nothing to anyone except to love one another; for he who loves his neighbor has fulfilled the law.
Romans 13:8

And why are you worried about clothing. Observe how the lilies of the field grow; they do not toil nor do they spin, yet I say to you that not even Solomon in all his glory clothed himself like one of these. But if God so clothes the grass of the field, which is alive today and tomorrow is thrown into the furnace, will He not much more clothe you?
Matthew 6:28-30

Do not worry then, saying, 'What will we eat?' or 'What will we drink?' or 'What will we wear for clothing?' For the Gentiles eagerly seek all these things; for your heavenly Father knows that you need all these things. But seek first His kingdom and His righteousness, and all these

things will be added to you.
Matthew 6:31-33

Give, and it will be given to you. They will pour into your lap a good measure – pressed down, shaken together, and running over. For by your standard of measure it will be measured to you in return.
Luke 6:38

Bear one another's burdens, and thereby fulfill the law of Christ.
Galatians 6:2

The apostles said to the Lord, "Increase our faith!" And the Lord said, "If you had faith like a mustard seed, you would say to this mulberry tree, 'Be uprooted and be planted in the sea.' and it would obey you.
Luke 17:5-6

Beware of practicing your righteousness before me to be noticed by them; otherwise you have no reward with your Father who is in heaven. But when you give to the poor, do not let your left hand know what your right hand is doing, so that your giving will be in secret; and your Father who sees what is done in secret will reward you.
Matthew 6:1, 3-4

CR80

REFLECTIONS ON FINANCES

_____

_____

_____

_____

_____

_____

_____

_____

_____

_____

_____

_____

_____

_____

_____

_____

_____

_____

_____

_____

_____

ॐ

FEAR

Father, I feel fearful of the unknown, of unexpected outcomes, and the future of [Name] and his/her loved ones. I know you have not given us a spirit of fear, but of power, love, and a sound mind. I pray my confidence is completely in you.

Forgive me for being fearful. Help me to abide in your perfect love which casts out fear. I know [Name], myself, and our families are protected by your promises, sustained by your Word, and upheld with your righteous right hand. I pray for a hedge of protection around my mind, body and spirit. Let your love and peace surround me and crowd out all fear.

Father, give me the words to encourage [Name]'s spirit when he/she is feeling overwhelmed by emotions like fear and discouragement. I pray the words we have heard regarding [Name]'s health will not cause fear in me or [Name] but that we remember you have the final say in all things and nothing happens but by your will.

I pray the lips and tongues of all those who surround [Name] bring life to him/her and their words are as uplifting as refreshing spring waters. Emotions can be unpredictable and are always changing like shifting shadows. But you God, never change. Bless [Name] to find stability in you. I pray the only fear [Name] knows is the burning, passionate, awe-inspiring fear of you, God.

VERSES FOR PRAYER, MEDITATION, & ENCOURAGEMENT

We have come to know and have believed the love which God has for us. God is love, and the one who abides in love abides in God, and God abides in him. There is no fear in love; but perfect love casts out fear, because fear involves punishment, and the one who fears is not perfected in love.
I John 4:16, 18

He shall say to them, 'Hear, O Israel, you are approaching the battle against your enemies today. Do not be fainthearted. Do not be afraid, or panic, or tremble before them, for the Lord your God is the one who goes with you, to fight for you against your enemies, to save you.'
Deuteronomy 20:3-4

For God has not given us a spirit of timidity, but of power and love and discipline.
2 Timothy 1:7

Be strong and courageous, do not be afraid or tremble at them, for the Lord Your God is the one who goes with you. He will not fail you or forsake you.
Deuteronomy 31:6

He will give his angels charge concerning you, To guard you in all your ways.
Psalm 91:11

He will not fear evil tidings; His heart is steadfast, trusting in the Lord. His heart is upheld, he will not fear, Until he looks with satisfaction on his adversaries.
Psalm 112:7-8

The Lord is my light and my salvation; Whom shall I fear? The Lord is the defense of my life; Whom shall I dread?
Psalm 27:1

The fear of the Lord is the beginning of knowledge; Fools despise wisdom and instruction.
Proverbs 1:7

ॐ

REFLECTIONS ON FEAR

_____
_____
_____
_____
_____
_____
_____
_____
_____
_____
_____
_____
_____
_____
_____
_____
_____
_____
_____
_____
_____
_____
_____

formula ornament

FAITH

Father, out of your glorious riches strengthen [Name] with power through your Spirit. Increase [Name]'s faith so that he/she may truly know whatever he/she asks for in your Name it will be given to him/her. If [Name] knew what was to come and the outcome of this journey, it would not be a journey of faith. I pray that when [Name] prays he/she will believe and not doubt. I know you will reward [Name] for earnestly seeking you. Thank you, Father.

Father, this journey will certainly test [Name]'s faith. I pray that not only will he/she withstand the test but come out as pure gold, persevering in all these trials. Because [Name] believes in you, Jesus, he/she will live and not die and he/she will see your glory. Because [Name] believes in you, he/she has victory and power. He/she will overcome this trial and come through it victorious. I thank you God, that [Name]'s faith is growing more and more. I pray that through this journey [Name]'s love for you will flourish.

Father, as your child, you have directed me not to lose heart, for you are making my inner self new every day. You have said these afflictions in my life, when compared to eternity, are fleeting. The suffering I am experiencing in this life, even now, is in fact giving rise to an eternal honor. Help me to view this new part of my life in the light of a Christ-like, eternal perspective. All the things I see now, all that is happening in my life and [Name]'s is temporary. Help me to understand moment to moment, the trials I am under-going are perfecting my faith and, by your power, are developing great perseverance and endurance. I pray that I stand upon your promises and withstand the test with the aid of your Holy Spirit.

Father, faith is the substance of things hoped for and the evidence of things not seen. Give me supernatural faith throughout this trial to believe and hope for the healing of [Name] and that you will strengthen all of us to withstand the attacks of the enemy.

My faith is increased by hearing and believing the Word of God. Give me the desire to read your Word regularly and help me to do so, so that my faith and knowledge in you may increase to not only withstand this trial but that it may be perfected. I want to seek you out and abide in you. I can't get through this on my own.

೧೩೮೦

VERSES FOR PRAYER, MEDITATION, & ENCOURAGEMENT

For the eyes of the Lord move to and fro throughout the earth that He may strongly support those whose heart is completely His.
2 Chronicles 16:8

Therefore I say to you, all things for which you pray and ask, believe that you have received them, and they will be granted you.
Mark 11:24

Truly, truly, I say to you, he who believes in Me, the works that I do, he will do also; and greater works than these he will do; because I go to the Father. Whatever you ask in My name, that will I do, so that the Father may be glorified in the Son. If you ask Me anything in My name, I will do it. If you love Me, you will keep My commandments.
John 14:12-15

For whatever is born of God overcomes the world; and this is the victory that has overcome the world – our faith. Who is the one who overcomes the world, but he who believes that Jesus is the Son of God?
1 John 5:4-5

Therefore we do not lose heart, but though our outer man is decaying, yet our inner man is being renewed day by day. For momentary, light affliction is producing for us an eternal weight of glory far beyond all comparison, while we look not at the things which are seen, but at the things which are not seen; for the things which are seen are temporal, but the things which are not seen are eternal.

2 Corinthians 4:16-18

Consider it all joy, my brethren, when you encounter various trials, knowing that the testing of your faith produces endurance. And let endurance have its perfect result, so that you may be perfect and complete, lacking in nothing.

James 1:1-3

Is anyone among you sick? Then he must call for the elders of the church and they are to pray over him, anointing him with oil in the name of the Lord; and the prayer offered in faith will restore the one who is sick, and the Lord will raise him up, and if he has committed sins, they will be forgiven him.

James 5:14-15

And He said to them, "Why are you afraid? Do you still have no faith?"

Mark 4:40

Then He touched their eyes, saying, "It shall be done to you according to your faith." And their eyes were opened.

Matthew 9:29-30

ೞ

REFLECTIONS ON FAITH

_____

_____

_____

_____

_____

_____

_____

_____

_____

_____

_____

_____

_____

_____

_____

_____

_____

_____

_____

_____

_____

_____

❧❦

DOUBT

Father, I am struggling considerably with numerous questions and few answers. I am in a place right now where I am doubting your promises; are you listening to my prayers? Will you answer? Are your promises even true, because I have yet to see the fruits of my prayers?

I know you are God. Your way is right, blameless, and pure. Although, many days I feel I am floundering in a sea of doubt and struggling with my faith—do not forsake me. Do not pass me by Lord. Do not let me wander from your commandments. Show yourself strong in my life and in my weaknesses. Help me to seek you with all my heart, especially at night, in the darkness, when I find it most difficult to find hope in your words.

Father, I trust you with everything I am. I believe in all of your promises. Help my unbelief! I am seeking you with all of my heart. Bring me back to the cross where Jesus died for my sins and carried out the greatest act of love and sacrifice.

Humble me before you. Give me the desire to read your Word again. Enlarge my understanding, increase my faith, and give me supernatural insights into your promises. I want to treasure your truths so that I might not sin against you. I want your words and praises to be on my lips. I want to pray and consider your Word with faith.

ೞ

VERSES FOR PRAYER, MEDITATION, & ENCOURAGEMENT

"But if You can do anything, take pity on us and help us!" And Jesus said to him, "'If You can?' All things are possible to him who believes." Immediately the boy's father cried out and said, "I do believe; help my unbelief."
Mark 9:22-24

But he must ask in faith without any doubting, for the one who doubts is like the surf of the sea, driven and tossed by the wind.
James 1:6

And He said to them, "Why are you troubled, and why do doubts arise in your hearts?
Luke 24:38

And blessed is he who does not take offense at Me.
Matthew 11:6

And He did not do many miracles there because of their unbelief.
Matthew 13:58

Therefore, keep up your courage, men, for I believe God that it will turn out exactly as I have been told.
Acts 27:25

Trust in the Lord with all your heart And do not lean on your own understanding. In all your ways acknowledge Him, And He will make your paths straight. Do not be wise in your own eyes; Fear the Lord and turn away from evil.
Proverbs 3:5-7

Those whom I love, I reprove, and discipline; therefore be zealous and repent.
Revelations 3:19

ॐ

REFLECTIONS ON DOUBT

೧೩೭

PEACE

Father, Jesus left His peace for all believers to inherit including *me. Your* peace is not something that should be difficult or elusive to find. It should accompany me wherever I go.

Instead, when I go into the hospital, treatment centers, or my loved one's home, I find myself worrying and doubting. My peace seems to flee. My soul has been fighting and wrestling with [Name]'s cancer diagnosis and the why's and how's and what's. I truly want to pursue you and rest in your perfect peace and stop being tossed around by the storm that swirls around me. I want my constant worrying and fighting to end. I want to be wrapped in tranquility that can only come from you and rest in the wholeness and fullness of your presence.

Yet, you are the Great I am, the author and finisher of my faith, the sole source of peace. Your peace means I am whole. Because it is from you, I know it is perfect and good. I can find no substitute for it on this earth.

Father, I am hungry and thirsty for you and your peace. I want to know you more and more so that I may find true spiritual rest. I want to be where you are, in your presence, where I will find comfort. Your presence is where prayers are heard, where there is forgiveness, where your cup never runs dry, where there are blessings, where I might see your glory, and where I can experience peace.

Help me not to be defined by external circumstances. Although my loved one is suffering and I feel pain because of it, I pray that I do not allow the precious gift of your peace to be stolen away. Though, I confess this has been very difficult for me and I need your help. Encourage my heart and minister to me, God. As long as I continue to stand on your promises, I should continue to experience your supernatural peace.

Father, I know [Name] is not alone. You promise in your Word when [Name] walks through the waters, he/she will not be swept away because you are with him/her You promise when [Name] walks through the fire he/she will not be burned and the flames will not set him/her ablaze because you are [Name]'s God. I know you are walking alongside [Name] right now. Please let [Name] feel your presence deeply. Let your peace, which surpasses all understanding, shield [Name] from all the anxieties he/she is facing.

Father, you have revealed to us many things in your Word so that we may have peace. You have told us to take heart and be encouraged. Jesus has overcome the world and stands alongside [Name] in battle. I know too that you are perfecting [Name]'s faith and mine so that we will not be lacking in anything.

Lord, you do *all* things well and that includes in the life of [Name] and myself. Bless [Name] with peace as he/she trusts in you and stands upon your promises.

I pray for peace for myself as well so that I may continue to pray for [Name] and encourage him/her in your Word and be a support to him/her in any way that you desire to use me. Help us both to believe your promises and know with our whole being that they are true.

Help us to love you more and more every day.

ඐ

VERSES FOR PRAYER, MEDITATION, & ENCOURAGEMENT

Peace I leave with you; My peace I give to you; not as the world gives do I give to you. Do not let your heart be troubled, nor let it be fearful.
John 14:27

Now may the Lord of peace Himself continually grant you peace in every circumstance. The Lord be with you all!
2 Thessalonians 3:16

These things I have spoken to you, so that in Me you may have peace. In the world you have tribulation, but take courage; I have overcome the world.
John 16:33

Consider it all joy, my brethren, when you encounter various trials, knowing that the testing of your faith produces endurance. And let endurance have its perfect result, so that you may be perfect and complete, lacking in nothing. But if any of you lacks wisdom, let him ask of God, who gives to all generously and without reproach, and it will be given to him. But he must ask in faith without any doubting, for the one who doubts is like the surf of the sea, driven and tossed by the wind.
James 1:2-6

Be anxious for nothing, but in everything by prayer and supplication with thanksgiving let your requests be made known to God. And the peace of God, which surpasses all comprehension, will guard your hearts and your minds in Christ Jesus.

Philippians 4:6-7

Yield now and be at peace with Him; Thereby good will come to you. Please receive instruction from His mouth And establish His words in your heart.

Job 22:21-22

࿒ఴఴ

REFLECTIONS ON PEACE

_____

_____

_____

_____

_____

_____

_____

_____

_____

_____

_____

_____

_____

_____

_____

_____

_____

_____

_____

_____

_____

♋

DEPRESSION

Father, depression feels like a mountain I cannot move.

A mountain that eclipses the promised light of your Son. A mountain so heavy, my very spirit is weighed down and stumbles about. This depression has prevented me from moving forward, thinking clearly, sleeping peacefully. . . . I am not able to give my family all of me. I'm not even sure who "me" is anymore. I'm simply existing and want so much to know where you are. When will you speak to me? Do you care? Are you listening? Hear my cry and remember me in my groanings and tears. Father, take notice of me and have mercy. Lift me out of this pit of darkness. Let me see your light again and the glory of your promises.

Father, I wait to hear from you. I wait to see you move.

I desperately need you to empower me to worship you while I wait; to praise you while I wait; to read your Word while I wait; to pray while I wait; to serve your people while I wait.

I remember your promises, God, and pray them to you now. I know you're listening, even when it doesn't feel like you are, for the shepherd hears the voice of his sheep. You have promised to help me move mountains. You have promised me I am victorious. Help me to stop struggling and fighting a battle you've already won through the power of your Son Jesus, the Good Shepherd.

Father, I'm exhausted and have run out of words. I don't know what else to pray, yet, I feel I must pray, I must draw near to you. Help me in this time to lean completely on you. You have given me authority in the name of Jesus, and by your power, to create change in and around my life. I can come to you and ask anything in the name of your Son and know you hear me and answer my prayers. I know the Spirit intercedes with heavenly groans that are deep and powerful, interpreting my prayers and making them acceptable in your sight. I don't have to worry that my words aren't perfect or even about the words themselves. My spirit cries unto you Lord. Deep calls unto deep. Thank you Lord. Thank you, that even in silence my spirit can abide in your love and be in communion with you knowing that you are God.

Father, there is nothing like depression to show me how broken I am and worthless in this world. Depression exposes my worldly delusions and ungodly expectations of myself and others. For there is no one who is able to fill this great crevice of despair; where nothing is accomplished and everything is swallowed up.

Though people may try, everyone falls short of bringing genuine joy to my heart, most of all myself. I cannot be motivated to do anything despite the notable efforts of friends and family to get me "involved". It feels as if my very mind and heart are working against me. This depression is a gaping wound that is inflamed and widening. It is a wound so raw it screams for a healing balm. My soul cries out for the perfect healing balm in Gilead.

Truly, it is only the saving blood of Christ that can rescue me from this pit. I am indeed in need of a Savior. Only a loving Savior, a merciful Savior, a Savior who was wounded, so that I might be healed, can drag me out of the miry clay, clean me off, and restore the brilliant shine of my spirit, when I first loved you. Restore me once more for your saving work. Revive me again. Use my hands and feet to accomplish your works and remind me once more of who I am in Christ.

Father, I know you haven't finished with me yet. You still have works for me to complete. Works you destined for me beforehand. Bless me to put my hands to the plow and work by the power and name of Jesus, especially when it's the last thing I want to do.

As you sent a violent earthquake to open the prison doors and break the prison chains for Paul and Silas, I need you to send a forceful shaking in my life to loose the chains of depression.

Thank you that your Son provided means for those chains to be broken two thousand years ago. You have redeemed me. Whom the Son sets free is free indeed.

Free me once more, Lord. Bring me forth into the time where I might go out in joy and be led by your peace. The time where the mountains burst into songs of joy before me and the trees of the field clap their hands. Bring me into the time where my light might break forth like the dawn. The time where my healing comes quickly, my righteousness goes before me, and my rear guard is the glory of the Lord.

VERSES FOR PRAYER, MEDITATION, & ENCOURAGEMENT

He found him in a desert land, And in the howling waste of a wilderness; He encircled him, He cared for him, He guarded him as the pupil of his eye. Like an eagle that stirs up its nest, That hovers over its young, He spread His wings and caught them, He carried them on His pinions. The Lord alone guided him, And there was no foreign god with him.
Deuteronomy 32:10-12

But we have this treasure in earthen vessels, so that the surpassing greatness of the power will be of God and not from ourselves; we are afflicted in every way, but not crushed; perplexed, but not despairing; persecuted, but not forsaken; struck down, but not destroyed; always carrying about in the body the dying of Jesus, so that the life of Jesus also may be manifested in our body. For we who live are constantly being delivered over to death for Jesus' sake, so that the life of Jesus also may be manifested in our mortal flesh. So death works in us, but life in you.
2 Corinthians 4:7-12

The Lord is near to the brokenhearted And saves those who are crushed in spirit. Many are the afflictions of the righteous, But the Lord delivers him out of them all.
Psalm 34:18-19

For whoever is joined with all the living, there is hope. . . .
Ecclesiastes 9:4

Then [Jesus] said to them, "My soul is deeply grieved, to the point of death; remain here and keep watch with Me." And He went a little beyond them, and fell on His face and prayed, saying, "My Father, if it is possible, let this cup pass from Me; yet not as I will, but as You will."
Matthew 26:38-39

The thief comes only to steal and kill and destroy; I came that they may have life, and have it abundantly.
John 10:10

I am the good shepherd; the good shepherd lays down His life for the sheep. I am the good shepherd, and I know My own and My own know Me, even as the Father knows me and I know the Father; and I lay down My life for the sheep. For this reason the Father loves Me, because I lay down My life so that I may take it again. No one has taken it away from Me, but I lay it down on My own initiative. I have authority to lay it down, and I have authority to take it up again. This commandment I received from My Father.
John 10: 11, 14-15, 17, 18

Why are you in despair, O my soul? And why are you disturbed within me? Hope in God, for I shall again praise Him, The help of my countenance and my God.
Psalm 43:5

Those who sow in tears shall reap with joyful shouting.
Psalm 126:5

Answer me quickly, O Lord, my spirit fails; Do not hide your face from me, Or I will become like those who go down to the pit. Let me hear your lovingkindness in the morning; For I trust in You; Teach me the way in which I should walk; For to You I lift up my soul.
Psalm 143:7-8

The LORD sustains all who fall And raises up all who are bowed down.
Psalm 145:14

For by grace you have been saved through faith; and that not of yourselves, it is the gift of God; not as a result of works, so that no one may boast. For we are His workmanship, created in Christ Jesus for good works, which God prepared beforehand so that we would walk in them.
Ephesians 2:8-10

ജ്ഞ

REFLECTIONS ON DEPRESSION

_____

_____

_____

_____

_____

_____

_____

_____

_____

_____

_____

_____

_____

_____

_____

_____

_____

_____

_____

_____

STRENGTH & COURAGE

Father, at times I feel very discouraged and disheartened. Especially when it seems as if we are taking two steps forward and three steps back. I pray you help me to lean not on my own understanding, but trust that your promises are true because you are not a man that you would lie. You have told me to cast all my cares upon you. You have told me that you see my struggles and you hear my cries. You promise to deliver me from all my troubles. In my weakness, you are strong. Uphold me with your righteous right hand.

Father, I pray your peace, which surpasses all understanding rests upon me, [Name], and all his/her loved ones. Help us to be anxious for nothing but bring everything to you in prayer: our discouragement, weaknesses, fears, and worry.

Open our eyes to clearly see all your gifts in our lives so that we may continue to give you thanks and praise your Name. Give us the courage to face the unknown days ahead. Days which are still filled, from sun-up to sundown, with good and perfect gifts from you, our Father of heavenly lights.

I pray, by your power, we have the courage to not worry about tomorrow, for tomorrow will take care of itself. Grant us the courage to allow you to be to us everything you have promised; to cast our burdens upon you so that you may sustain us; to not fear because you are our God; to wait when you say wait; to praise when you say praise; to go when you say go; to meditate upon what is lovely and good and excellent despite the ugliness that surrounds us.

Thank you for being our strength and shield; for being our fortress and protecting us in the shadow of your wings.

ॐ

VERSES FOR PRAYER, MEDITATION, & ENCOURAGEMENT

The Lord is my strength and my shield; My heart trusts in Him, and I am helped; Therefore my heart exults, And with my song I shall thank Him. The Lord is their strength, And He is a saving defense to His anointed.
Psalm 28:7-8

Be strong and let your heart take courage, All you who hope in the Lord.
Psalm 31:24

[T]o keep me from exalting myself, there was given me a thorn in the flesh, a messenger of Satan to torment me— to keep me from exalting myself! Concerning this I implored the Lord three times that it might leave me. And He has said to me, "My grace is sufficient for you, for power is perfected in weakness." Most gladly, therefore, I will rather boast about my weaknesses, so that the power of Christ may dwell in me.
2 Corinthians 12:7-9

Do not fear, for I am with you; Do not anxiously look about you, for I am your God. I will strengthen you, surely I will help you, Surely I will uphold you with My righteous right hand.
Isaiah 41:10

Cast your burden upon the LORD and He will sustain you;
He will never allow the righteous to be shaken.
Psalm 55:22

For this reason also, since the day we heard of it, we have
not ceased to pray for you and to ask that you may be
filled with the knowledge of His will in all spiritual wisdom
and understanding, so that you will walk in a manner
worthy of the Lord, to please Him in all respects, bearing
fruit in every good work and increasing in the knowledge
of God; strengthened with all power according to His
glorious might, for the attaining of all steadfastness and
patience; joyously giving thanks to the Father, who has
qualified us to share in the inheritance of the saints in
Light.
Colossians 1:9-12

Rejoice in the Lord always; again I will say, rejoice! Let
your gentle spirit be known to all men. The Lord is near.
Be anxious for nothing, but in everything by prayer and
supplication with thanksgiving let your requests be made
known to God.
Philippians 4:4-6

೦೩೮೦

REFLECTIONS ON STRENGTH AND COURAGE

_____

_____

_____

_____

_____

_____

_____

_____

_____

_____

_____

_____

_____

_____

_____

_____

_____

_____

_____

_____

ℭℜℰℭℭ

HOPELESSNESS

Father, thank you for the many blessings and miracles you have done in my life. Your Word exhorts me to remember your wonders and your deeds. I especially want to remember not only what you have done for your people throughout the ages but what you have done for *me* and *my* family. Help me to remember the times I've drawn near to you where I felt such sweet peace; the times where I felt I could praise you for hours – days even, in joyful tears and shouts of thanksgiving and dancing for how you had blessed me; the times where it seemed we were so close and I could talk to you about anything and hear you speaking in return.

Help me especially to remember those times now; now, when I can hardly recall what hope feels like, or what it feels like to live without anxiety. When I look at what [Name] and our loved ones are going through I feel hopeless and anxious. I feel the whole world is against us and there is no hope. How can we stand against this cancer when it has seeped into and ravaged [Name]'s body and even our lives? Revive hope within me Lord, as only you can. Fill me once more with joy and peace and strengthen me so that hope does not flee again.

Father, you urge me to cast all my cares upon you and you will sustain me; you will never let me fall. I want to bring all my cares to you and leave them at your feet. Lord, I feel hopelessness because of the diagnosis the doctors have given [Name]. Therapies and surgeries haven't been effective. The weight of medical bills and even co-pays are crushing. How will we get through this? [Name]'s condition deteriorates rapidly. How can I be hopeful? And should [Name] pass, I do not know how we will endure. God, there is no hope to be found anywhere on earth to restore my soul.

I am thirsty, burdened and weak in faith. I do believe in you, but help my unbelief.

I praise the name of the Lord God Almighty, that because of your Son, I can lay all my concerns at your altar and expect that you will fill me with *all* joy and peace, and by the power of the Holy Spirit I may abound in hope.

I cannot see a way out. But who hopes for what they can see? You are the light in the darkness, the calm in the storm and my ever present help in trouble. Embolden me to rejoice in you with all my heart and soul.

ᘓᘓ

VERSES FOR MEDITATION, PRAYER, AND ENCOURAGEMENT

Though the fig tree should not blossom And there be no fruit on the vines, Though the yield of the olive should fail And the fields produce no food, Though the flock should be cut off from the fold And there be no cattle in the stalls, Yet I will exult in the Lord, I will rejoice in the God of my salvation.
Habakkuk 3:17-18

Now may the God of hope fill you with all joy and peace in believing, so that you will abound in hope by the power of the Holy Spirit.
Romans 15:13

God is our refuge and strength, A very present help in trouble.
Psalm 46:1

"But if You can do anything, take pity on us and help us!" And Jesus said to him, "'If you can?' All things are possible to him who believes." Immediately the boy's father cried out and said, "I do believe; help my unbelief."
Mark 9:22-24

And not only this, but we also exult in our tribulations, knowing that tribulation brings about perseverance; and perseverance, proven character; and proven character, hope; and hope does not disappoint, because the love of

God has been poured out within our hearts through the
Holy Spirit who was given to us.
Romans 5:3-5

Finally, brethren, whatever is true, whatever is honorable,
whatever is right, whatever is pure, whatever is lovely,
whatever is of good repute, if there is any excellence and
if anything worthy of praise, dwell on these things.
Philippians 4:8

Therefore we do not lose heart, but though our outer
man is decaying, yet our inner man is being renewed day
by day. For momentary, light affliction is producing for us
an eternal weight of glory far beyond all comparison. . . .
2 Corinthians 4:16-17

For in hope we have been saved, but hope that is seen is
not hope; for who hopes for what he already sees? But if
we hope for what we do not see, with perseverance we
wait eagerly for it. In the same way the Spirit also helps
our weakness; for we do not know how to pray as we
should, but the Spirit Himself intercedes for us with
groanings too deep for words; and He who searches the
hearts knows what the minds of the Spirit is, because He
intercedes for the saints according to the will of God.
Romans 8:24-27

Therefore, do not throw away your confidence, which has
a great reward. For you have need of endurance, so that
when you have done the will of God, you may receive
what was promised.
Hebrews 10:35-36

ൟ

REFLECTIONS ON HOPELESSNESS

_____

_____

_____

_____

_____

_____

_____

_____

_____

_____

_____

_____

_____

_____

_____

_____

_____

_____

_____

_____

_____

ॐ

PERSEVERING

Father, at times this trial seems too great to overcome. Often I feel I am fighting a battle on my own, swimming against a current that is too strong for me, praying I'll somehow survive. Yet, as I pray I remember your Son. Jesus struggled much under the heaviness of your plan for his life. He sweat blood because of the intensity of his prayers the night before he was taken. Yet, Jesus endured his darkest night in communion with you, never leaving your side and you never leaving his. Only you can strengthen a man to withstand such evils of this world. Only you can gird my faith, and steady my heart and my hands to persevere to the end.

Thank you for the awe-inspiring example of Jesus to willingly bear the cross and die on it for everyone, including those who would reject him. I want to willingly bear the cross you have given to me in this life, remaining in constant communion with you. Wherever I am found wanting, fill me up. Your grace is sufficient for me to keep placing one foot in front of the other and following your Spirit wherever He leads.

Father, in the same manner strengthen [Name] to withstand this heavy trial. Draw close to him/her and support him/her to endure to the very end. Allow him/her to overcome with thanksgiving and rejoicing. Remind [Name], if he/she is faithful you will award him/her the crown of life. His/Her name will be in the mouth of Jesus as he confesses before you, our Father, that [Name] is yours.

Bless [Name] to hold fast to what he/she has so he/she will be a pillar in your kingdom forever. Like our biblical ancestors, who had such great faith, help [Name] to understand that we do not receive what is promised in this life. But you have prepared a city for him/her and riches far greater than he/she could ask or imagine. Let [Name] be a faithful steward of what you have given into his/her hands, so that by the power of Jesus he/she may overcome this trial and finish his/her race with joy and thanksgiving.

FURTHER VERSES FOR PRAYER, MEDITATION, & ENCOURAGEMENT

For you have need of endurance, so that when you have done the will of God, you may receive what was promised. For yet in a very little while, He who is coming will come, and will not delay. But My righteous one shall live by faith; And if he shrinks back, My soul has no pleasure in him.
Hebrews 10:36-38

For our struggle is not against flesh and blood, but against the rulers, against the powers, against the world forces of this darkness, against the spiritual forces of wickedness in the heavenly places. Therefore, take up the full armor of God, so that you will be able to resist in the evil day, and having done everything, to stand firm.
Ephesians 6:12-13

The LORD is near to the brokenhearted And saves those who are crushed in spirit. Many are the afflictions of the righteous, But the LORD delivers him out of them all.
Psalm 34:18-19

I know your deeds. Behold, I have put before you an open door which no one can shut, because you have a little power, and have kept My word, and have not denied My name.
Revelations 3:8

I am coming quickly; hold fast what you have, so that no one will take your crown. He who overcomes, I will make him a pillar in the temple of My God, and he will not go out from it anymore; and I will write on him the name of My God, and the name of the city of My God, the new Jerusalem, which comes down out of heaven from my God, and My new name.
Revelations 3:11-12

Now faith is the assurance of things hoped for, the conviction of things not seen. For by it the men of old gained approval. By faith we understand that the worlds were prepared by the word of God, so that what is seen was not made out of things which are visible. All these died in faith, without receiving the promises, but having seen them and having welcomed them from a distance, and having confessed that they were strangers and exiles on the earth. For those who say such things make it clear that they are seeking a country of their own. And indeed if they had been thinking of that country from which they went out, they would have had opportunity to return. But as it is, they desire a better country, that is, a heavenly one. Therefore God is not ashamed to be called their God; for He has prepared a city for them. And all these, having gained approval through their faith, did not receive what was promised, because God had provided something better for us, so that apart from us they would not be made perfect.
Hebrews 11:1-3, 13-16, 39-40

For I consider that the sufferings of this present time are not worthy to be compared with the glory that is to be revealed to us.
Romans 8:18

REFLECTIONS ON PERSEVERING

_____

_____

_____

_____

_____

_____

_____

_____

_____

_____

_____

_____

_____

_____

_____

_____

_____

_____

_____

_____

_____

_____

೫೫

FINISHING THE RACE (DEATH) & HEAVENLY RICHES

Father, [Name] has passed. Despite all my prayers for healing and the prayers of so many loved ones, friends, family, and even those that did not know [Name] personally but prayed on his/her behalf, you chose in your wisdom and even your mercy not to heal [Name] of cancer in this life.

For [Name] this is a great victory because he/she finished the race with your Name on his/her lips and in his/her heart. The enemy was indeed out for [Name]'s soul, but he/she persevered and stood strong upon your Word and in your promises until the very end.

The enemy tried to make [Name] stumble and fall. He tried to make [Name] question your love and your promises. The enemy would have seen [Name] curse you before death, but [Name] did not. You did not rescue [Name]'s body from death but you rescued his/her very soul. And now, [Name] will worship and serve you in eternity. Though, I am grieving, I praise you now that one day I will meet [Name] again on streets of gold, lit radiantly by the glory of the Lamb.

Father, your Word says at times you take the righteous to protect them from future evil and to keep their eyes from seeing disaster. Perhaps this was your reason for bringing [Name] home to you in spite of our fervent prayers for more time.

As a seed must die to bring forth a tree that bears fruit for generations to come, I know the life and death of [Name] will bring forth spiritual seed in your kingdom for generations to come.

I can see, even now, how through [Name]'s illness you taught me to serve in humility, patience, to trust in you in my darkest moments, to pray like I never have before, and draw near to you with an intentionality and intensity that was necessary to survive. I'm certain I am not the only one who has grown spiritually and whose spiritual gifts you used to build your kingdom in eternity through [Name]'s battle.

Thank you God for using [Name] as an essential building stone for erecting your kingdom that will endure forever.

ᏣᎳ

VERSES FOR MEDITATION, PRAYER, AND ENCOURAGEMENT

Precious in the sight of the Lord Is the death of His godly ones.
Psalm 116:15

Jesus said to her, "I am the resurrection and the life; he who believes in Me will live even if he dies, and everyone who lives and believes in Me will never die. Do you believe this?"
John 11:25-26

Christ Jesus . . . abolished death and brought life and immortality to light through the gospel . . . .
2 Timothy 1:10

But when this perishable will have put on the imperishable, and this mortal will have put on immortality, then will come about the saying that is written, "Death is swallowed up in victory. O death, where is your victory? O death, where is your sting?" The sting of death is sin, and the power of sin is the law; but thanks be to God, who gives us the victory through our Lord Jesus Christ. Therefore, my beloved brethren, be steadfast, immovable, always abounding in the work of the Lord, knowing that your toil is not in vain in the Lord.
1 Corinthians 15:54-58

For I am convinced that neither death, nor life, nor angels, nor principalities, nor things present, nor things to come, nor powers, nor height, nor depth, nor any other created thing, will be able to separate us from the love of God, which is in Christ Jesus our Lord.

Romans 8:38

Therefore, behold, I will gather you to your fathers, and you will be gathered to your grave in peace, and your eyes will not see all the evil which I will bring on this place.

2 Kings 22:20

For the righteous man is taken away from evil, He enters into peace; They rest in their beds, Each one who walked in his upright way.

Isaiah 57:1-2

He Who overcomes, and he who keeps My deeds until the end, to Him I will give authority over the nations; and he shall rule them with a rod of iron, as the vessels of the potter are broken to pieces, as I also have received authority from My Father; and I will give him the morning star.

Revelations 2:26-27

But we do not want you to be uninformed, brethren, about those who are asleep, so that you will not grieve as do the rest who have no hope. For if we believe that Jesus died and rose again, even so God will bring with Him those who have fallen asleep in Jesus. For this we say to you by the word of the Lord, that we who are alive and remain until the coming of the Lord, will not precede those who have fallen asleep. For the Lord Himself will

descend from heaven with a shout, with the voice of the archangel and with the trumpet of God, and the dead in Christ will rise first. Then we who are alive and remain will be caught up together with them in the clouds to meet the Lord in the air, and so we shall always be with the Lord. Therefore comfort one another with these words.
1 Thessalonians 4:13-18

If Christ is in you, though the body is dead because of sin, yet the spirit is alive because of righteousness. But if the Spirit of Him who raised Jesus from the dead dwells in you, He who raised Christ Jesus from the dead will also give life to your mortal bodies through His Spirit who dwells in you. The Spirit Himself testifies with our spirit that we are children of God, and if children, heirs also, heirs of God and fellow heirs with Christ, if indeed we suffer with Him so that we may also be glorified with Him.
Romans 8:10-11, 16-17

But the saints of the Highest One will receive the kingdom and possess the kingdom forever, for all ages to come.
Daniel 7:18

He who overcomes, I will grant to him to sit down with Me on My throne, as I also overcame and sat down with My Father on His throne.
Revelations 3:21

⚝

REFLECTIONS ON FINISHING THE RACE
AND HEAVENLY RICHES

_____
_____
_____
_____
_____
_____
_____
_____
_____
_____
_____
_____
_____
_____
_____
_____
_____
_____
_____
_____
_____
_____

∽

SPIRITUAL DARKNESS & JESUS' LIGHT

Father, I am caught in the middle of a tempest. The storm swirls around me drowning out your words of comfort and promise threatening to destroy my faith. I cannot hear your voice or see you working in my life. I am desperate to find something beautiful in this storm, to see the light of your promises, to hope again, to believe in you once more with my whole being. I feel completely insecure and uncertain. Help my unbelief, God. Revive me according to your Word. Restore me back to life; set me back into motion, enfolded in your light, love, peace and goodness. Renew my mind. Pour your life into me and banish my feelings of uselessness, hopelessness and worthlessness. Validate me. Vindicate me.

Father, I am cloaked in darkness. I'm having a burdensome time coming to terms with the passing of [Name]. I wonder if you heard my countless prayers? If there was ever a prayer I sought fervently for an answer – those were it: my prayers for healing. But healing didn't come in this life. I hardly feel like praying any more. I ask— what's the point? What other prayer could matter more than the one I uttered thousands of times, the one I implored, begged and pleaded at Heaven's gates daily and nightly with tears and supplication? Even with thanksgiving, praise, faith and hope. Did I not do everything you required of me? Did I not ask? Did I not knock? Now, when I pray, my little faith is obscured by distrust and even cynicism. Words do not come because I hesitate with disbelief that you will even answer. Are you even listening? Do you really answer prayer? If so – where were you when I needed you?

Father, I come to you now because I must. As Job has said, I will continue to bring my case before you-- though you slay me, I must hope. I must pray. I am, after all, *your* child. And deep calls unto deep. My soul longs for you even if my mind wants to turn away from you. My flesh and spirit are in an ever present struggle. I don't know how to move forward. I've fought with such dread and disquiet. My grief is a wearisome burden. I'm angry, Lord. I have lost my desire to read your Word and hardly know how to pray anymore. I'm not even sure if I hear you speaking to me. I feel as though I am truly walking through the valley of the shadow of death, where I am met with nothing but stony muteness.

I know when I pray you hear me, because you have promised you hear the prayers of your people. You have the power to call me out of darkness into your glorious light. To speak things that are not, as though they were; speaking life from death. Call me out, Father, into your glorious light. Speak life to me.

Father, in your Word the Spirit of God hovers and moves in the never-ending darkness, right before you speak light into the world. You promise that I can't get lost in the darkness, because darkness is as light to you and you will find me. I recognize my feelings are not to be trusted right now. I feel lost, I feel alone; I wonder if you see me. . . .

Hover in my spirit so that I might feel you moving. Find me, Lord. Find me in all my pain and suffering. Find me and speak light back into my heart and my life. You promise you will never leave me or forsake me. You promise that when I cry out, you will hear me because I am yours.

Command the darkness over me to flee, so that I will not be overcome. Empower me to follow you, especially now, so that I will never walk in darkness and will have the light of life. Help me to cling to the truth of who your Son is and the insurmountable power in his Name, that is available to me.

Jesus was revealed as the light of the world. I need Jesus to shine in my soul. Let his light shine on me in the fullness of its glory so that the darkness cannot withstand it. As the brilliance of understanding, by the power of Jesus, works in my soul, swallow up all fear, doubt, anger, and disbelief. Bring this carnal world into a Christ-like focus, Lord. Empower me to walk in the light, as you are in the light. Let my soul find rest, for you have been good to me.

Please open my spiritual eyes and provide depth of perception to see the scourge of cancer in [Name's] life for what it truly is *today*: Defeated.

I know [Name] is in paradise with you. He/she has been changed from glory to glory. He/she is no longer in pain or suffering. He/she now has his/her inheritance in you and is fully sanctified, justified, and glorified.

You have told me to stop weeping, because you have overcome. You alone hold the keys to death and you alone unlocked that door many years ago so that death has no victory. Thank you that I am yours. Let me rejoice in you, Father, all the days of my life.

VERSES FOR MEDITATION, PRAYER, AND ENCOURAGEMENT

Then Jesus again spoke to them, saying, "I am the Light of the world; he who follows Me will not walk in the darkness, but will have the Light of life."
John 8:12

If I say, "Surely the darkness will overwhelm me, And the light around me will be night," Even the darkness is not dark to You, And the night is as bright as the day. Darkness and light are alike to you.
Psalm 139:11-12

All things came into being through Him, and apart from Him nothing came into being that has come into being. In Him was life, and the life was the Light of men. The Light shines in the darkness, and the darkness did not comprehend it.
John 1:3-5

Do not fear, for I have redeemed you; I have called you by name; you are Mine! When you pass through the waters, I will be with you; And through the rivers, they will not overflow you. When you walk through the fire, you will not be scorched, Nor will the flame burn you. For I am the Lord your God, The Holy One of Israel, your Savior. . . .
Isaiah 43:1-3

"Arise, shine; for your light has come, And the glory of the Lord has risen upon you. For behold, darkness will cover the earth And deep darkness the peoples; But the Lord will rise upon you And His glory will appear upon you. Nations will come to your light, And kings to the brightness of your rising. . . Then you will see and be radiant, And your heart will thrill and rejoice. . . ."
Isaiah 60:1-3, 5

Return to your rest, O my soul, For the Lord has dealt bountifully with you. For You have rescued my soul from death, My eyes from tears, My feet from stumbling. I shall walk before the Lord In the land of the living.
Psalm 116: 7-9

Wake up, and strengthen the things that remain, which were about to die; for I have not found your deeds completed in the sight of My God.
Revelations 3:2

For He rescued us from the domain of darkness, and transferred us to the kingdom of His beloved Son, in whom we have redemption, the forgiveness of sins.
Colossians 1:13-14

If it is disagreeable in your sight to serve the Lord, choose for yourselves today whom you will serve: whether the gods which your fathers served which were beyond the River, or the gods of the Amorites in whose land you are living; but as for me and my house, we will serve the Lord.
Joshua 24:15

ल৪ৎ

ACKNOWLEDGEMENTS

I praise God for enabling me to write this book even when it was difficult; I praise Him for taking so much hurt and making it beautiful for me and prayerfully for you.

To my husband
Scott Curry,
Your love, support, and encouragement have been indispensable in helping me get through this journey;

To my parents and brother
Tommy and Theresa Newsom and *T.L. Newsom II*
who are always giving to others of themselves;

To *Tony Jefferson*, (Jackie's former Fiancé); *Sarah E. Rosenberry*; *Charmaine Anderson*;
Pastor *Cleveland Thompson* of
Emmanuel Missionary Baptist Church in Colorado Springs who preached a powerful message of "He Does All Things Well" at Jackie's Home-Going Service. A message that has remained with me. Thank you Pastor Thompson for serving God with such obedience and passion;
My **Abounding Grace Ministries** family of New York City and especially to
Pastors Rick and Arlene Del Rio,
who rallied around my family with much prayer and unparalleled support. In you all I have a family for life!;
To our new church family, **Solid Rock Christian Center** of Colorado Springs and
Pastors Ben and Wanda Anderson
for their genuinely loving hearts and support!

And to my Sister Twin,
Jackie –
Thank you. . .

Sister Twin, Identical Twin

Sister twin, identical twin, together for 29 years;
Lots of memories, lots of laughter, and maybe a few tears.

Remember Teddy and Squeaky? Our stuffed animals we adored?
We wanted to have hot dogs in heaven; Jesus and just us four.

Tender twin, warmhearted twin, we were never apart,
Cheerful twin, joyful twin, your smiles warmed our hearts.

Remember when you said to mom, "I asked God for a little brother"?
Mom turned to you and said, "Nu-uh, we're not having another!"

Well, you and God got really close, and clearly you prayed well
Much to Mom and Dad's surprise…his name would be T.L.

Treasured twin, priceless twin, children you always cherished.
The joy of children in our lives with you never perished.

Remember when you said to me, "You're having twins,
I prayed"?
"No you didn't, take it back!" I yelled with false dismay.

"It's in the hands of God right now, there's nothing I can
do."
And sure enough inside of me, there was not one, but
two.

Christian twin, praying twin, you got your prayers right
through.
Just look at our little brother and my two precious boos.

Before you passed, for six long days, you didn't eat a
thing.
Then suddenly you asked a friend for food that she
would bring.

"Two large hot dogs, not from hospice!" Clearly, you
demanded.
And after ordering the food, two hot dogs you were
handed.

You didn't eat the hot dogs though and I think I do know
why:
You remembered a dream of long ago, you prepared to
say goodbye.

The Son whispered in your ear "Jackie you've finished
your race."
"At my table I have for you a very special place."

"I see you've ordered us some food, with hot dogs I'm content."
And Jackie gave her last goodbye and peacefully she went.

Dancing twin, singing twin, I know who you're eating with today.
Laughing, smiling, cartwheeling, it's a perfect heavenly day.

Loving twin, living twin, my sister I'll never forget.
Life is but a vapor. . . I'll join you. . . just not yet.

BY STEPHANIE CURRY
IN REMEMBRANCE OF MY TWIN

JACQUELINE ARLENE NEWSOM
MAY 01, 2014

Stephanie wants to hear from you.
Please send your comments about the book to
prayingtobreakchains@yahoo.com

If you would like to schedule Stephanie Curry as a speaker,
please contact her at the following email address:
prayingtobreakchains@yahoo.com

45117851R00078

Made in the USA
San Bernardino, CA
01 February 2017